Mediterranean Breakfast Sandwich Maker Cookbook for Beginners

1001-Day Classic and Tasty Recipes to Enjoy Mouthwatering Sandwiches, Burgers, Omelets and More | Help you Lose Weight and Achieve A Healthy Lifestyle

Jems Helth

© Copyright 2021 Jems Helth - All Rights Reserved.

In no way is it legal to reproduce, duplicate, or transmit any part of this document by either electronic means or in printed format. Recording of this publication is strictly prohibited, and any storage of this material is not allowed unless with written permission from the publisher. All rights reserved.

The information provided he rein is stated to be truthful and consistent, in that any liability, regarding inattention or otherwise, by any usage or abuse of any policies, processes, or directions contained within is the solitary and complete responsibility of the recipient reader. Under no circumstances will any legal liability or blame be held against the publisher for any reparation, damages, or monetary loss due to the information herein, either directly or indirectly.

Respective authors own all copyrights not held by the publisher.

Legal Notice:

This book is copyright protected. This is only for personal use. You cannot amend, distribute, sell, use, quote or paraphrase any part of the content within this book without the consent of the author or copyright owner. Legal action will be pursued if this is breached.

Disclaimer Notice:

Please note the information contained within this document is for educational and entertainment purposes only. Every attempt has been made to provide accurate, up-to-date and reliable, complete information. No warranties of any kind are expressed or implied. Readers acknowledge that the author is not engaging in the rendering of legal, financial, medical or professional advice.

By reading this document, the reader agrees that under no circumstances are we responsible for any losses, direct or indirect, which are incurred as a result of the use of information contained within this document, including, but not limited to, errors, omissions, or inaccuracies.

Table of contents

Introduction 5
Chapter 1: Basics of Mediterranean Diet 6
    What Is the Mediterranean Diet? 6
    The History of The Mediterranean Diet 6
    Benefits of The Mediterranean Diet 7
Chapter 2: Basics of Breakfast Sandwich Maker 9
    Why Do You Need It? 9
    How Does It Work? 10
    How to Use The Breakfast Sandwich Maker? 11
    Cleaning the Appliance 12
    Troubleshooting 13
    Additional Tips for Best Results 14
Chapter 3: 21-Day Meal Plan 16
Chapter 4: Classic Breakfast Sandwiches and Omelets 21

    Sausage Omelet with Paprika and Cheese 21
    Pepperoni Pizza Omelet 23
    Croissant Sandwich with Sausage, Egg, and Cheddar 24
    Ham and Cheese Egg Biscuit Sandwich 25
    Cheddar and Bacon Omelet 26
    Eggs Benedict Sandwich 27
    Chili Cheesy Omelet with Bacon 28
    Classic Bagel Sandwich with Bacon, Egg, and Cheese 29
    Muffin Sandwich with Egg, Ham, and Cheese 30
    Cheddar Sandwich with Prosciutto ... 31

Chapter 5: Vegetarian Breakfast Sandwiches and Omelets 32

    Huevos Rancheros on Tortilla 32
    Egg White Sandwich with Spinach and Goat's 34
    Mustardy Egg Muffin Melt 36
    Everything Bagel Mushroom and Mozzarella Sandwich 38
    Classic Grilled Cheese Sandwich 39
    Tomato and Pepper Omelet with Mozzarella 40
    Apple and Brie Croissant Sandwich .. 42
    Herbed Omelet with Cream Cheese and Cheddar 43

Chapter 6: Pork Sandwiches 45

    Pork Roast and Egg Sandwich 45
    Pork Muffin Sandwich 47
    Apple and Pork Muffin Melt 48
    Spicy Pork and Pimento Sandwich 49
    Hot Pork Sausage and Srambled Egg Sandwich 51
    Pork and Egg Tortilla Open Sandwich 52

Veggie and Pork Mayo Sandwich ...... 53　Pulled Pork Sandwich 55

Chapter 7: Chicken and Turkey Sandwiches 56

The Ultimate Chicken, Spinach and Mozzarella Sandwich 56
Spicy Turkey and Sausage Sandwich .. 58
Chicken and Bacon Paprika Sandwich 60
Pita Bread Chicken Sandwich 62
Turkey Salsa Melt 64
Ground Turkey Taco Cups 65
Cheesy Chicken Waffle Sandwich 66
Moist Leftover Chicken Biscuit 67

Chapter 8: Fish and Seafood Sandwiches 68

Tilapia and Pimento Dijon Sandwich 68
Yogurt and Dill Open Cod Sandwich 69
Tuna and Corn Muffin Sandwich 70
Canned Salmon and Bacon Pickle Sandwich 71
Salmon and Pistachio Melt 73
Sour Cream and Crab Cake Sandwich 74
Fish Finger Sandwich 75
Salsa and Shrimp Biscuit Sandwich ... 76

Chapter 9: Gluten-Free Sandwiches 77

Gluten-Free Crispy Grilled Cheese and Bacon Sandwich 77
Avocado Sandwich with Egg, Ham and Cheese 79
Mexican Gluten-Free Pork Sandwich 80
Almond Pancake with Egg and Prosciutto 82
Almond Flour Waffle and Sausage Sandwich 83
Cornbread and Egg Sandwich 84
Corn Bowl with Tomato, Bacon, and Cheese 85
Gluten-Free Smoked Salmon and Cream Cheese Sandwich 86

Chapter 10: Beef Sandwiches and Burgers 87

Classic Hamburger 87
Beef and Veggies Bagel Sandwich 89
Chili Sandwich 91
Sausage and Biscuit 92
Bolognese Cup 93
Beef, Waffle, and Egg Sandwich 94
Cheesy Beef and Egg Sandwich 95
The Ultimate 4-Minute Cheeseburger 97

Chapter 11: Desserts and Snacks 99

Chocolate Croissant 99
Crunchy Nutella and Strawberry Bagel 100
Berry Pancake 101
Peanut Butter Waffle with Banana .. 102
Olive and Cheese Snack 103
Cinnamon Apple Biscuit 104
Pizza Snack 105
Tropical Croissant with Sugar 106

Conclusion 107

Introduction

It can be really frustrating to have to think of what to throw together every single morning. Making healthy Mediterranean breakfast should be a breeze, not extra work. All the recipes written in this book are easily understandable and carefully selected. You will find delicious and healthy Mediterranean breakfast recipes for every single day.

Are you a Mediterranean breakfast lover? Do you want to revolutionize the way you make your breakfast? Do you want a breakfast maker that you could total control over and is easy to clean? The Mediterranean breakfast sandwich maker is the answer to all the questions raised.

This book, Mediterranean Breakfast Sandwich Maker Cookbook for Beginners: including 1001 mouth-watering recipes that are quick and easy to prepare, but offer amazing taste at the same time for your choosing. Mediterranean breakfast is easier than ever with these delicious recipes.

Chapter 1: Basics of Mediterranean Diet

What Is the Mediterranean Diet?

When studied historically the Mediterranean diet can be tied to a specific region or era. But scientifically proven the Mediterranean diet taken a much universally place in human history. Due to its unique approach to food consumption, it brings more balance to our diet and fills our plate with a healthy nutritional meal in a proportionate amount. It is an innate human need to consume food of all sorts, ranging from protein-rich meats to the fiber loaded vegetables, and fruits and the carb filled grains. So, this diet only works in light of such need. Its emphasis more on clean fats and healthy oils for daily consumption. The diet carried its name from its origin, which is rooted in the region around the Mediterranean Sea. People from those places were more reliant on seafood, fresh vegetables, fruits, olive oil, and whole grains. Their approach rightly guided the world to a nutrient-rich meal plan.

The greatest thing about the Mediterranean diet is it does not only guarantee good health, but it comes with so much flavor, aroma, and colors for our platters. Unlike, other restrictive diets, the Mediterranean diet is much more open and flexible. It suggests so many delectable options for every taste palate that it is easy for anyone to adopt. Over the course of time, the Mediterranean diet has significantly evolved according to different regions and culinary cultures. Today, it manages to prevent and cure several life-threatening diseases.

The History of The Mediterranean Diet

The Mediterranean diet that exists today originated from the stretches of Greece and Italy. Different classes of those societies individually contributed to the formation of this diet. There was a great inclination towards the eating of white omega rich meat including all seafood. Along with that, they use to consume lots of vegetables, fruits, and grains in some amount. The typical food patterns of the people in those areas were adopted readily by many due to the diversity of the nutrients the Mediterranean pyramid has provided. Over the years it existed as a culinary tradition, it was not until 1975 when American biologist Ansel keys and Margaret key collaborated to publicize the Mediterranean diet as a health-oriented meal plan. However, its widespread recognition came late in the 1990s. Studies regarding the benefits of this diet were conducted in Madrid and Naples; the objective data obtained revealed significant results. This study confirms the wide-ranging effects of the Mediterranean diet over people's health which were predicted decades ago. Later scientists came up with their different versions of the Mediterranean diet, but the one which was readily adopted was given by Walter Willet and his colleagues in mid-1990s. This approach was closest to the naturally evolved Mediterranean diet. It suggests a similar pattern of food intake as the people from ancient Greece did.

Benefits of The Mediterranean Diet

A healthy diet can do miracles no medicine can guarantee. Mediterranean diet is no less than miraculous if we acknowledge the great benefits it brings to human health. Besides accelerating the rate of metabolism and detoxifying the body from harmful oxidants, this diet can deal with a range of mental and physical ailments including cancer, cardiovascular disorders, and Parkinson, etc.

1. Prevent Alzheimer and Parkinson:

Both Parkinson and Alzheimer are neural disorders which result from the toxic build up in the brain and damage caused by it. The Mediterranean diet has shown unbelievable effects over the patients of Parkinson and Alzheimer, and they all experience improved mental functioning because of this diet plan.

2. Fights Against Cardiovascular Diseases:

All the cardiovascular diseases are linked with high blood cholesterol levels or weakening of the cardiac muscles. With the Mediterranean diet, such threats can be fought due to its good fat content. It does not allow the accumulation of bad fats and toxins in the body while keeping the metabolism active and running all the time.

3. Lowers Bad Cholesterol:

The olive oil based Mediterranean diet is free from all the saturated fats. Resultantly it is low on bad cholesterol. This form of cholesterol is responsible for blocking the blood vessels and causes a high blood cholesterol level.

4. High Life Expectancies:

Good diet and longevity have a very real connection. The better you eat, the healthier you stay. When you eat everything and balance, it can guarantee a long life. This fact is happened to be true for people consuming a Mediterranean diet, and therefore it is prescribed to everyone looking for higher life expectancy.

5. Aids Cancer Treatment:

Another curse of the current age is incurable cancer and the like diseases. Where most of the medicinal and chemical therapies fail to cure the disease, a change in diet have proven miraculous for most of the cancer patients. Mediterranean diet has been proven the most beneficial in this regard. People who are already consuming this diet shows about a sixty percent lesser tendency of developing cancer than the people who don't consume it.

Chapter 2: Basics of Breakfast Sandwich Maker

So you've seen all those commercials that promote this magical appliance and decided it was time for you to buy one. Congratulations! As soon as you start preparing breakfast in the Breakfast Sandwich Maker, you will see that this gadget casts a shadow over your traditional morning meals.

Fully cooked meal ready in 5 minutes? What's not to like? If you don't like making breakfast or don't have the time for it, this appliance will help you eat healthily without sacrificing your time.
Read on to learn the ultimate tips on using the Breakfast Sandwich Maker.

Why Do You Need It?

There is a lot to love about this breakfast sandwich maker, but the things that most users find to be the most beneficial are:

Breakfast in Under 5 Minutes... Without Actually Making It

No more rushing the most important meal of the day, no more gobbling down unhealthy pre-made and packaged choices. With this amazing appliance, you can enjoy your breakfast in under 5 minutes, without having to stir, sauté, or flip in front of the stove. While the Breakfast Sandwich Maker does its job, you get to prepare your coffee, fix your hair, get dressed or do whatever it is your doing on a hectic morning. All you need to do is simply assemble the ingredients, set the timer, and that's it!

One-Dish Meal

Okay, let's say you want to enjoy a breakfast sandwich, but do not own the Breakfast Sandwich Maker. You will need to toast the buns/bread, fry the egg separately, maybe even warm your pre-cooked meat, and then assemble the ingredients. That will require that you use a toaster or a roasting pan, another pan for the fried egg, a spatula, etc. Which leaves you with a bunch of dishes for washing. Who has time for that in the morning? This appliance will both toast your eggs, warm the ingredients, and fry the eggs at the same time. And you will only have one dish for washing.

Evenly Cooked

When preparing breakfast sandwiches the traditional way, it is pretty hard to achieve a consistent crispiness and even temperature. Why? Because you don't do it all at once. You will need to separately fry your eggs, toast your breads, melt your cheeses, etc. Some will be cooked more than the others, the bread may go cold while you whip up your eggs, etc. This appliance though, does it all at ones.

Your job is only to assemble the ingredients and it will cook the egg perfectly, toast the bread to ideal crispiness, melt the cheese, and leave you with a center that is delectably warm. You cannot achieve this evenness another way. And you get it all in under 5 minutes which is why it is said that the Breakfast Sandwich Maker makes one high-class breakfast.

Affordable

Unlike other fancy cooking appliances that costs hundreds of dollars, the Breakfast Sandwich Maker will not break your bank. In fact, you can get it in just $24.99. And the best part? You don't have to buy two appliances so that you and your loved one can enjoy warm breakfast together. Breakfast Sandwich Maker allows you to cook two separate sandwiches at the same time. And the price? Just $39.99.

You Can Make Omelets

But, besides for being great for making sandwiches, the Breakfast Sandwich Maker is also a unit that will help you perfectly fry eggs and cook omelets as well. Just add the eggs without any bread or other additions, and you will have a first-class omelet in just 3-4 minutes.

How Does It Work?

If you've been wondering whether the appliance works as smoothly as in the commercial – yes, you can be sure it does. The process couldn't be more straightforward – you just pile up your ingredients and that's it:

1. Arrange half bun at the bottom.
2. Add a slice of cheese and/or some meat that is pre-cooked (ham, bacon, sausage, etc.)
3. Crack an egg into the barrier.
4. Top with the other half of bun.
5. Close and cook for 4-5 minutes.

How to Use The Breakfast Sandwich Maker?

The overall process of using the appliance couldn't be simpler. To do it properly, just follow these steps:

1. Plug the appliance's cord into an outlet. At that point, the **red** power light should be glowing.
2. While the appliance preheats, spray its rings with nonstick cooking spray, but do it lightly.
3. Make sure that the unit is closed and that the cooking plate is between the greased rings.
4. Once the sandwich maker preheats, you will be able to notice the **green** power light growing. Keep in mind that this will go on and off just as the light for your oven does. Also, remember that this is only related to the temperature and does not indicates when your breakfast is ready.
5. Lift the cover of the appliance carefully, using the handles. With mittens, lift up the top ring and the cooking plate as well.
6. Now, you are ready to assemble the sandwich.
7. The bottom half of your bun should be placed onto the bottom plate. Arrange your preferred ingredients on top.
8. Now, move the top ring and lower the cooking plate.
9. Crack an egg onto the plate. For best results, pierce the yolk with a toothpick or a fork. Note that you don't have to use a whole egg only. You can also add scrambled eggs or only egg whites.
10. Top with the top bun.

11. Put the lid on and cook your sandwich for about 4 or 10 minutes.
12. Once the cooking is done, rotate the cooking plate clockwise all the way through.
13. Carefully lift the ring and cover by holding the bottom handle. Use mittens.
14. Do NOT use metal utensils, but transfer the sandwich to a plate with the help of a plastic, wooden, or silicone spatula.
15. Unplug and let cool.

Be sure to:

- Have your ingredients ready before starting to assemble the sandwich.
- Keep the cover closed when preheating. The cooking plate and rings should be in place.
- Check to see if the cooking plate is in place before preheating or even adding the food.

Cleaning the Appliance

What good would cooking breakfast under 5 minutes do to us if we are supposed to wash its parts later by hand? No, the ring of the Breakfast Sandwich Maker is dishwasher safe. Here is how you can clean the appliance thoroughly:

1. You need to have your appliance disconnected before cleaning. NEVER immerse the base, cord, or plug of the sandwich maker in water. It is recommended that you always unplug your unit after the cooking is done, so make sure to follow that advice.
2. Once your unit cools down, remove its ring by holding the bottom handle to open, and simply lift it straightly.
3. If you are washing it by hand, make sure not to use scouring pads, wool, or any abrasive cleaners. If you are washing it in the dishwasher, make sure not to use the "Sani" setting as its program and cycle temperature may cause some damages to the ring.
4. Unfortunately, the bottom and top heating plates cannot be removed. However, their cleaning is really simple. Just grab a soapy soft sponge and wipe the plates with

it. Then, wipe it again with a sponge soaked in water to sort of "rinse" it, and that's it. The cooking plates are non-stick, so you really don't need more than a simple wipe to clean them thoroughly. Let the plates dry thoroughly.
5. To place the ring back inside, just make sure that the ring's tabs and the hinge's openings are aligned, and then simply lower it into its place.
6. Clean the outside of the unit with a damp cloth.

Troubleshooting

Just like with any other appliance, once you start using the Hamilton Beach Breakfast Sandwich Make you may stumble upon some issues. But worry not, because those problems are usually a product of improper handling. Read on to see what the most troubleshooting issues are and how to fix them:

Eggs are Undercooked and the Bread is not Crispy Enough

Okay, so, you cannot expect the same cooking time for small and extra large eggs. If you use particularly large eggs, allow an extra minute for them to cook.

If you are using frozen ingredients, obviously, you will need an extra minute or so for the bread to be done.

The Ingredients Stick to the Ring or the Cooking Plates

While the appliance is non-stick, you should always grease it with cooking spray before using. Melted cheese can get baked-on.

The Bread is Overly Browned

Sugars or ingredients high in fat content may cause the bread to darken too quickly. Cook your eggs without the bread for a couple of minute before actually adding the bread, if that is the case.

Low or Slow Heating

Wait for the green light that indicates that the unit is preheated. The correct temperature time is achieved within 5-7 minutes, which is enough for you to assemble the ingredients in the meantime.

If the heating is low, it usually means that the unit is overfilled – use less ingredients.

Check the cooking plate and see if it is rotated the right way.

Also, make sure that the unit is closed when preheating.

In between sandwiches, allow for 2 minutes of preheating time.

Eggs Leak Out

Again, the unit is probably overfilled. Make sure not to use many ingredients and do not press down on the cover.

The Cover Rises During Cooking

Sometimes, especially if cooking a large scrambled egg, the egg whisked into it may cause the cover to rise. Just leave it as it is, do NOT press on it.

Additional Tips for Best Results

Here are some additional tips that will up your cooking with the Breakfast Sandwich Maker:

- Use round breads, buns, and bagels for best results. You can trim the edges of a normal loaf bread to fit perfectly, but that is not a requirement. You can also just place the bread as it is and smash a bit to fit. It might get darker around the edges, but it will still be perfectly toasted.
- Do not smoosh. Place the lid gently and do not press on it; it is not a panini maker. Pressure is not required for ideal cooking here.
- It is all in the timing. For perfectly cooked breakfast, find the perfect cooking time. Set a kitchen timer or do it on the phone, but make sure to cook for the ideal time.
- Taking a peek is allowed. If you are not sure whether your sandwich is ready or not, simply open the lid and take a peek, just like you'd do with your oven.

- Always use mittens when opening the cover of the unit. The surface is hot and there can be steam escaping so getting burn is a possibility you need to be aware of.

Chapter 3: 21-Day Meal Plan

Yes, your mornings, (and afternoons and evenings!) will be a lot simpler when you have the HBBSM (Breakfast Sandwich Maker) on hand. But, why take my word for it? Follow this simple meal plan for 21 days, and see how you can incorporate these sandwiches into your eating schedule. I promise a significant difference is about to be discovered.

Day 1

Breakfast: HBBSM Cheddar and Bacon

Lunch: Creamy Mushroom Soup

Dinner: HBBSM Classic Hamburger

Dessert: A piece of Fruit Cake

Day 2

Breakfast: HBBSM Huevos Rancheros on Tortilla

Lunch: Grilled Chicken (accompanied with a small portion of rice and green salad)

Dinner: HBBSM Apple and Pork Muffin Melt

Dessert: Two Scoops of Favorite Ice Cream

Day 3

Breakfast: HBBSM Egg Benedict Sandwich

Lunch: Cesar Salad

Dinner: Beef Stew with a slice of bread

Dessert: HBBSM Apple and Cinnamon Biscuit

Day 4

Breakfast: HBBSM Pepperoni Pizza Omelet

Lunch: Tomato Soup with a slice of bread

Dinner: Pork Roast with Potatoes and Carrots

Dessert: 1 Chocolate Bar

Day 5

Breakfast: Oatmeal or Granola

Lunch: HBBSM Pita Bread Chicken Sandwich

Dinner: Spaghetti Carbonara

Dessert: HBBSM Tropical Croissant with Sugar

Day 6

Breakfast: HBBSM Mustardy Egg Muffin Melt

Lunch: Macaroni and Cheese

Dinner: HBBSM Bolognese Cup

Dessert: Frozen Yogurt

Day 7

Breakfast: HBBSM Classic Bagel Sandwich with Bacon, Egg, and Cheese

Lunch: Clear Chicken Soup with a piece of toast

Dinner: Steak and Mashed Potatoes

Dessert: A piece of Chocolate Cake

Day 8

Breakfast: Favorite Morning Smoothie

Lunch: HBBSM Tuna and Corn Muffin Sandwich

Dinner: Chili with Green Salad

Dessert: Fruit Bowl topped with whipped cream

Day 9

Breakfast: HBBSM Chilli Cheesy Omelet with Bacon

Lunch: Lobster Salad

Dinner: HBBSM Beef and Veggies Bagel Sandwich

Dessert: One brownie

Day 10

Breakfast: HBBSM Crosisant Sandwich with Sausage, Egg, and Cheddar

Lunch: Fish Fillet with Rice

Dinner: HBBSM Sausage and Biscuit

Dessert: A piece of fruit

Day 11

Breakfast: HBBSM Classic Grilled Cheese Sandwich

Lunch: HBBSM Yogurt and Dill Open Cod Sandwich

Dinner: Lamb Stew

Dessert: Apple Pie

Day 12

Breakfast: Oatmeal or Granola

Lunch: HBBSM Avocado Sandwich with Egg, Ham, and Cheese

Dinner: Chicken and Zucchini Risotto

Dessert: A small piece of Cheesecake

Day 13

Breakfast: HBBSM Everything Bagel Mushroom and Mozzarella Sandwich

Lunch: Creamy Tomato and Basil Soup with some bread

Dinner: Pork Chops with Roasted Potatoes

Dessert: Tiramisu

Day 14

Breakfast: HBBSM Sausage Omelet with Paprika and Cheese

Lunch: Cauliflower Rice with Cheese and Veggies

Dinner: HBBSM The Ultimate 4-minute Cheeseburger

Dessert: Cherry Pie

Day 15

Breakfast: Smoothie with Seeds and Nuts

Lunch: HBBSM Salmon and Pistachio Melt

Dinner: Rice and Meat by choice

Dessert: Poached Pears

Day 16

Breakfast: HBBSM Ham and Cheese Egg Biscuit Sandwich

Lunch: Crab Cakes with salad

Dinner: Pasta Primavera

Dessert: Fruit Cake Bar

Day 17

Breakfast: HBBSM Pepperoni Pizza Omelet

Lunch: HBBSM Apple and Brie Croissant Sandwich

Dinner: Chicken Curry with Rice

Dessert: A piece of Chocolate Cake

Day 18

Breakfast: Oatmeal with fruit

Lunch: HBBSM Chicken and Bacon Paprika Sandwich

Dinner: Mashed Potatoes with Meat by choice and Green Beans or Peas

Dessert: 1 cupcake

Day 19

Breakfast: HBBSM Sausage and Biscuit

Lunch: HBBSM Chocolate Croissant

Dinner: Fish Fillet with favorite side dish

Dessert: A piece of fruit

Day 20

Breakfast: HBBSM Crunchy Nutella and Strawberry Bagel

Lunch: HBBSM Turkey Salsa Melt

Dinner: Beef Stew

Dessert: 1 plain Vanilla Muffin

Day 21

Breakfast: HBBSM Gluten-Free Smoked Salmon and Cream Cheese Sandwich

Lunch: Clear Soup with one slice of Bread and a small portion of Green Salad on the side

Dinner: Spaghetti Bolognese

Dessert: 1 Chocolate Bar

Chapter 4: Classic Breakfast Sandwiches and Omelets

Sausage Omelet with Paprika and Cheese

Preparation Time: 5 minutes
Cooking Time: 4 minutes
Servings: 1

Ingredients:

- 1 ounce cooked breakfast Sausage, chopped
- 2 Eggs
- 1 ounce shredded Cheese
- ¼ tsp Smoked Paprika
- 1 tsp chopped Onion
- Salt and Pepper, to taste

Method:

1. Preheat the sandwich maker and grease it with cooking spray.
2. Whisk the eggs in a bowl and add the onion to them. Season with paprika, salt and pepper.
3. Pour half of the egg mixture to the bottom ring.
4. Top with the cheese and sausage.
5. Lower the top ring and the cooking plate.
6. Pour the remaining eggs into the cooking plate.
7. Close the unit and cook for about 4 minutes.
8. Rotate the plate clockwise and carefully open. Transfer the omelet to a plate.
9. Serve as desired and enjoy!

Nutritional Information per Serving:

- Calories 371
- Total Fats 28.5g
- Carbs 2g

- Protein 25.5g
- Fiber: 0.1g

Pepperoni Pizza Omelet

Preparation Time: 5 minutes
Cooking Time: 4 minutes
Servings: 1

Ingredients:

- 2 Eggs
- 1 ounce Pepperoni, sliced
- 2 tsp Tomato Puree
- 1 ounces shredded Cheese
- Salt and Pepper, to taste

Method:

1. Preheat and grease the sandwich maker.
2. Whisk the eggs in a bowl and season with some salt and pepper.
3. Stir in the tomato puree.
4. When the green light appears, pour half of the eggs to the bottom ring of the unit.
5. Top with the cheese and pepperoni.
6. Lower the cooking plate and the top ring, and pour the remaining eggs into the cooking plate.
7. Close and cook for 4 minutes.
8. Rotate the plate clockwise and transfer to a plate.
9. Serve and enjoy!

Nutritional Information per Serving:

- Calories 392
- Total Fats 30g
- Carbs 3.2g
- Protein 25.6g
- Fiber: 0.6g

Croissant Sandwich with Sausage, Egg, and Cheddar

Preparation Time: 5 minutes
Cooking Time: 5 minutes
Servings: 1

Ingredients:

- 5 Slices of Cooked Sausage
- 1 Egg
- 1 slice Cheddar
- 1 Croissant
- 2 tsp Mayonnaise
- Salt and Pepper, to taste

Method:

1. Preheat and grease the sandwich maker.
2. Cut the croissant in half and spread the mayonnaise over the cut-side of each half.
3. Place one half of the croissant with the cut-side up in the bottom ring.
4. Top with the cheddar and sausage.
5. Lower the cooking plate and crack the egg into it. Season with salt and pepper.
6. Top with the second croissant half, placing it with the cut-side down.
7. Close the unit and cook for 4 to 5 minutes.
8. Rotate clockwise carefully, and transfer to a plate.
9. Serve and enjoy!

Nutritional Information per Serving:

- Calories 580
- Total Fats 41.5g
- Carbs 27g
- Protein 24g
- Fiber: 1.5g

Ham and Cheese Egg Biscuit Sandwich

Preparation Time: 5 minutes
Cooking Time: 5 minutes
Servings: 1

Ingredients:

- 1 Biscuit, halved
- 2 Red Pepper Rings
- 1 Egg
- 1 Ham Slice
- 1 slice American Cheese
- Salt and Pepper, to taste

Method:

1. Preheat the sandwich maker and grease with some cooking spray.
2. When the green light appears, place the bottom half of the biscuit in the bottom ring.
3. Top with the cheese, ham, and pepper rings.
4. Lower the cooking plate and crack the egg into it. Season with some salt and pepper.
5. Add the top biscuit half on top and close the appliance.
6. Cook for 5 minutes.
7. Open carefully by sliding clockwise and transfer with plastic spatula to a plate.
8. Serve and enjoy!

Nutritional Information per Serving:

- Calories 270
- Total Fats 15.5g
- Carbs 14g
- Protein 17.7g
- Fiber: 0.5g

Cheddar and Bacon Omelet

Preparation Time: 5 minutes
Cooking Time: 3-4 minutes
Servings: 1

Ingredients:

- 2 Large Eggs
- 2 tbsp cooked and crumbled Bacon
- 2 tbsp shredded Cheddar Cheese
- Salt and Pepper, to taste

Method:

1. Preheat your Breakfast Sandwich Maker and grease it with some cooking spray.
2. Beat the eggs lightly.
3. When the green lights turn on, open the unit, and add half of the whisked eggs into the bottom ring.
4. Top with the cheese and bacon.
5. Add the rest of the eggs to the cooking plate.
6. Close and cook for 3 to 4 minutes.
7. Rotate the handle clockwise to open.
8. Remove with a plastic or silicone spatula.
9. Serve and enjoy!

Nutritional Information per Serving:

- Calories 348
- Total Fats 26g
- Carbs 1.2 g
- Protein 24.5g
- Fiber: 0g

Eggs Benedict Sandwich

Preparation Time: 5 minutes
Cooking Time: 4 to 5 minutes
Servings: 1

Ingredients:

- 4 Baby Spinach Leaves
- 1 English Muffin
- 1 Slice Canadian Bacon
- 1 tbsp Hollandaise Sauce
- 1 Egg, lightly whisked

Method:

1. Preheat the Breakfast Sandwich Maker and spray it with some cooking spray.
2. Split the muffin in half and add one half to the bottom ring.
3. Top with the baby spinach and bacon.
4. Lower the cooking plate and add the egg to it.
5. Top with the remaining muffin half and close the unit.
6. Let cook for 4 to 5 minutes.
7. Turn the handle clockwise and open carefully.
8. Transfer the sandwich with a plastic spatula to a plate.
9. Drizzle the Hollandaise Sauce on top.
10. Enjoy!

Nutritional Information per Serving:

- Calories 330
- Total Fats 14.7g
- Carbs 31g
- Protein 19g
- Fiber: 2.5g

Chili Cheesy Omelet with Bacon

Preparation Time: 5 minutes
Cooking Time: 4 ½ minutes
Servings: 1

Ingredients:

- 2 Eggs, whisked
- 1/4 Red Chili, chopped
- ¼ tsp Garlic Powder
- 1 slice cooked and crumbled Bacon
- 1 ounce Mozzarella Cheese, shredded
- Salt and Pepper, to taste

Method:

1. Preheat and grease the sandwich maker.
2. Season the eggs with salt, pepper, and garlic powder.
3. When the green light appears, add half of the whisked eggs to the bottom ring.
4. Place the mozzarella, bacon, and chilli on top.
5. Add the remaining eggs to the cooking plate.
6. Close and let cook for 4 ½ minutes.
7. Open by sliding clockwise and transfer the omelet carefully to a plate.
8. Serve and enjoy!

Nutritional Information per Serving:

- Calories 277
- Total Fats 18g
- Carbs 2.8g
- Protein 24.7g
- Fiber: 2.8g

Classic Bagel Sandwich with Bacon, Egg, and Cheese

Preparation Time: 5 minutes
Cooking Time: 5 minutes
Servings: 1

Ingredients:

- 1 Plain Bagel
- 1 slice American Cheese
- 1 large Egg
- 1 slice of Bacon, precooked

Method:

1. Preheat and grease the sandwich maker.
2. Cut the bagel in half and place the bottom half to the bottom ring of the unit.
3. Top with the bacon and cheese.
4. Lower the cooking plate as well as the top ring, and crack the egg open into the cooking plate.
5. Place the top half of the bagel on top.
6. Close the unit and wait for about 4 to 5 minutes before transferring to a plate with the use of a plastic, wooden, or silicone spatula.
7. Serve and enjoy!

Nutritional Information per Serving:

- Calories 389
- Total Fats 14.5g
- Carbs 39g
- Protein 24g
- Fiber: 1.6g

Muffin Sandwich with Egg, Ham, and Cheese

Preparation Time: 5 minutes
Cooking Time: 5 minutes
Servings: 1

Ingredients:

- 1 slice Cheese
- 1 English Muffin
- 1 slice Canadian Bacon
- 1 Egg, scrambled

Method:

1. Preheat and grease the sandwich maker.
2. Cut the English muffin in half and place one half with the spilt-side up into the bottom ring.
3. Top with the bacon and cheese.
4. Now, lower the cooking plate and add the egg inside.
5. Close and let cook for 4-5 minutes.
6. Slide clockwise to open using mittens.
7. Remove the sandwich carefully and transfer to a plate.
8. Serve and enjoy!

Nutritional Information per Serving:

- Calories 357
- Total Fats 17g
- Carbs 26g
- Protein 24g
- Fiber: 2g

Cheddar Sandwich with Prosciutto

Preparation Time: 5 minutes
Cooking Time: 3 ½ minutes
Servings: 1

Ingredients:

- 2 slices White Bread
- 2 slices Cheddar Cheese
- 1 Prosciutto Slice
- 1 tbsp Butter

Method:

1. Preheat the sandwich maker and grease it with some cooking spray.
2. Trim the bread slices or cut in a circle with a cookie cutter, to make sure they fit inside.
3. Spread the butter onto the slices.
4. When preheated, place one bread circle in the bottom ring with the butter-side up.
5. Top with the prosciutto and cheese.
6. Add the second bread slice with the butter side down.
7. Close and let the sandwich cook for about 3 ½ minutes.
8. Open by sliding out the cooking plate clockwise.
9. Transfer to a plate and enjoy!

Nutritional Information per Serving:

- Calories 495
- Total Fats 27g
- Carbs 39.7g
- Protein 27.5g
- Fiber: 6g

Chapter 5: Vegetarian Breakfast Sandwiches and Omelets

Huevos Rancheros on Tortilla

Preparation Time: 5 minutes
Cooking Time: 4 minutes
Servings: 1

Ingredients:

- 1 Mini Wheat Tortilla
- 1 tsp chopped Red Pepper
- 1 Egg
- 2 tsp chopped Onion
- 1 tbsp Beans
- 2 tsp Salsa
- ¼ cup shredded Cheddar Cheese
- Salt and Pepper, to taste

Method:

1. Preheat and grease the sandwich maker.
2. With a cookie cutter, cut out the tortilla if needed so it can fit inside the sandwich maker.
3. Whisk the egg in a bowl or directly in the cooking plate, and season with salt and pepper.
4. Stir in the onion and red pepper.
5. Place the tortilla into the bottom ring.
6. Place the beans and cheese on top.
7. Lower the cooking plate and pour the egg inside.
8. Close the unit and cook for 4 minutes.
9. Rotate clockwise to open and transfer to a plate, carefully, with a plastic spatula.
10. Top with the salsa.

11. Serve and enjoy!

Nutritional Information per Serving:

- Calories 360
- Total Fats 21g
- Carbs 16g
- Protein 18g
- Fiber: 2.5g

Egg White Sandwich with Spinach and Goat's

Preparation Time: 5 minutes
Cooking Time: 5 minutes
Servings: 1

Ingredients:

- 1 Whole Wheat English Muffin
- 2 Egg Whites
- 1 ounce Goat's Cheese
- 1 tbsp chopped Spinach
- 1 tbsp chopped Pepper
- Salt and Pepper, to taste

Method:

1. Preheat and grease the sandwich maker.
2. Whisk the egg whites and season with some salt and pepper.
3. Cut the muffin in half.
4. Place one half in the bottom of the unit, with the cut-side up.
5. Top with the cheese, spinach, and pepper.
6. Lower the cooking plate and ring and pour the egg whites inside.
7. Top with the second half of the muffin, this time with the cut-side down.
8. Close the unit and cook for 5 minutes.
9. Rotate clockwise to open and transfer to a plate with a plastic or wooden spatula.
10. Serve and enjoy!

Nutritional Information per Serving:

- Calories 255
- Total Fats 7.7g
- Carbs 29.5g
- Protein 19.5g

- Fiber: 5.5g

Mustardy Egg Muffin Melt

Preparation Time: 5 minutes

Cooking Time: 4 minutes

Servings: 1

Ingredients:

- 1 English Muffin
- 2 ounces shredded Cheddar Cheese
- 2 tsp Yellow Mustard
- 1 Egg
- Salt and Pepper, to taste
- 1 tsp chopped Parsley

Method:

1. Preheat and grease the sandwich maker with cooking spray.
2. Cut the English muffin in half and brush the insides with the mustard.
3. Whisk the egg and season it with salt and pepper. Stir in the chopped parsley.
4. When the green light appears, place half of the muffin in the bottom ring, with the cut-side down.
5. Top with the cheese.
6. Lower the top ring and cooking plate, and pour the whisked egg into the plate.
7. Top with the second muffin half, keeping the cut-side down.
8. Close and cook for 4 minutes.
9. Rotate clockwise and open.
10. Transfer the sandwich to a plate and enjoy!

Nutritional Information per Serving:

- Calories 435
- Total Fats 25g
- Carbs 27g

- Protein 26g
- Fiber: 2.3g

Everything Bagel Mushroom and Mozzarella Sandwich

Preparation Time: 5 minutes
Cooking Time: 3 minutes
Servings: 1

Ingredients:

- 1 Everything Bagel
- 3 tbsp marinated Mushrooms
- 1 ½ ounce shredded Mozzarella Cheese
- 1 tsp Mustard
- 1 tsp chopped Parsely

Method:

1. Preheat the sandwich maker and spray the inside of the unit with cooking spray.
2. Cut the bagel in half and lightly brush the insides with mustard.
3. When the green light appears, place one half of the bagel into the bottom ring, with the cut-side up.
4. Sprinkle the cheese over and top with the mushrooms and parsley.
5. Lower the cooking plate and top ring and add the second bagel half with the cut-side down.
6. Close and cook for 3 minutes.
7. Slide out the plate by rotating clockwise, open, and transfer to a plate.
8. Enjoy!

Nutritional Information per Serving:

- Calories 365
- Total Fats 9.7g
- Carbs 52g
- Protein 17g
- Fiber: 3.7g

Classic Grilled Cheese Sandwich

Preparation Time: 5 minutes
Cooking Time: 4 minutes
Servings: 1

Ingredients:

- 2 slices of Bread
- 1 ounce shredded Mozzarella
- 1 ounce shredded Gouda
- 2 tsp Butter

Method:

1. Preheat the Hamilton Beach Breakfast Sandwich and grease it with some cooking spray.
2. Cut the bread slices so that they can fit inside the sandwich maker.
3. Spread 1 tsp of butter onto each of the slices.
4. Place one slice of the bread into the bottom ring with the butter-side down.
5. Top with the cheeses.
6. Lower the top ring and add the second slice, placing it with the butter-side up.
7. Close the appliance and cook for about 4 minutes, or less if you want it less crispy.
8. Slide out by rotating clockwise. Lift the cover carefully and transfer the sandwich to a plate.
9. Serve and enjoy!

Nutritional Information per Serving:

- Calories 453
- Total Fats 25g
- Carbs 39g
- Protein 21g
- Fiber: 6g

Tomato and Pepper Omelet with Mozzarella

Preparation Time: 5 minutes
Cooking Time: 4-5 minutes
Servings: 1

Ingredients:

- 2 Eggs
- 1 ounce shredded Mozzarella Cheese
- 2 Tomato Slices, chopped
- 1 ½ tbsp chopped Red Pepper
- 1 tsp chopped Parsley
- ¼ tsp Onion Powder
- ¼ tsp Garlic Powder
- Salt and Pepper, to taste

Method:

1. Preheat and grease the sandwich maker.
2. Beat the eggs and season with onion powder, garlic powder, and salt and pepper.
3. Stir in the parsley.
4. Pour half of the eggs inside the bottom ring.
5. Top with the mozzarella, chopped pepper and tomatoes.
6. Lower the top ring and cooking plate and pour the rest of the eggs into the plate.
7. Close and cook for about 4 to 5 minutes.
8. Rotate the handle clockwise, lift to open, and transfer the omelet to a plate.
9. Serve and enjoy!

Nutritional Information per Serving:

- Calories 240
- Total Fats 26g
- Carbs 4.2g

- Protein 19.3g
- Fiber: 0.7g

Apple and Brie Croissant Sandwich

Preparation Time: 5 minutes
Cooking Time: 4 minutes
Servings: 1

Ingredients:

- 2 Apple Slices
- 1 ounce Brie, crumbled
- 1 Croissant
- 2 tsp Cream Cheese

Method:

1. Preheat and grease the sandwich maker.
2. Cut the croissant in half and spread one teaspoon of cream cheese over each half.
3. When the green light appears, place one of the croissant halves into the bottom ring, with the cut-side up.
4. Top with the apple slices and brie.
5. Lower the top ring and cooking plate and place the other croissant half inside.
6. Close and cook for 4 minutes.
7. Turn the handle clockwise, open, and transfer to a plate.
8. Serve and enjoy!

Nutritional Information per Serving:

- Calories 369
- Total Fats 23g
- Carbs 29g
- Protein 11g
- Fiber: 2g

Herbed Omelet with Cream Cheese and Cheddar

Preparation Time: 5 minutes

Cooking Time: 4-5 minutes

Servings: 1

Ingredients:

- 1 ounce Shredded Cheddar
- 2 Eggs
- ¼ tsp Garlic Powder
- 2 tsp Cream Cheese
- 1 tsp chopped Parsley
- 1 tsp chopped Cilantro
- ½ tsp chopped Dill
- Pinch of Smoked Paprika
- Salt and Pepper, to taste

Method:

1. Preheat and grease the sandwich maker.
2. Whisk the eggs and season with salt, pepper, garlic powder, and paprika.
3. Stir in the cream cheese, parsley, and cilantro.
4. When the green light appears, pour half of the eggs into the bottom ring of the unit.
5. Top with the shredded cheddar and dill.
6. Lower the top ring and cooking plate, and pour the remaining eggs inside.
7. Close the unit and let cook for 4 to 5 minutes.
8. Rotate the handle clockwise and transfer to a plate.
9. Serve as desired and enjoy!

Nutritional Information per Serving:

- Calories 290

- Total Fats 22g
- Carbs 1.8g
- Protein 20.5g
- Fiber: 0.1g

Chapter 6: Pork Sandwiches

Pork Roast and Egg Sandwich

Preparation Time: 5 minutes
Cooking Time: 4 minutes
Servings: 1

Ingredients:

- 1 slice of Pork Roast, about 2 ounces
- 1 Egg
- 2 Whole Wheat Bread Slices
- 2 tsp Butter
- 1 ounce American Cheese
- ¼ tsp Smoked Paprika
- Salt and Pepper, to taste

Method:

1. Preheat the unit and spray it with some cooking spray.
2. Brush each bread slice with butter.
3. Place one of the slices inside the bottom ring, with the butter-side down.
4. Top with the pork slice and place the cheese on top.
5. Lower the cooking plate and crack the egg into it.
6. Sprinkle the paprika over and season to taste.
7. Close the appliance and cook for 4 minutes.
8. Rotate the handle clockwise and lift to open.
9. Serve and enjoy!

Nutritional Information per Serving:

- Calories 425
- Total Fats 27g

- Carbs 30g
- Protein 22g
- Fiber: 3g

Pork Muffin Sandwich

Preparation Time: 5 minutes
Cooking Time: 5 minutes
Servings: 1

Ingredients:

- 1 Frozen Pork Pattie
- 1 English Muffin
- 1 Slice Cheddar Cheese
- 1 tsp Dijon Mustard

Method:

1. Preheat and grease the sandwich maker.
2. Cut the muffin in half and brush one of the halves with the mustard.
3. Place the muffin half onto the bottom ring with the mustard-side up.
4. Top with the frozen pattie and place the cheese on top.
5. Lower the top ring and add the second half with the cut-side down.
6. Cook for full 5 minutes.
7. Open by rotating clockwise and lifting the lid.
8. Transfer to a plate and enjoy!

Nutritional Information per Serving:

- Calories 490
- Total Fats 27g
- Carbs 25g
- Protein 33g
- Fiber: 2g

Apple and Pork Muffin Melt

Preparation Time: 5 minutes

Cooking Time: 4 minutes

Servings: 1

Ingredients:

- 2 ounces cooked Pork, chopped
- 2 slices Granny Smith Apple
- 1 English Muffin
- 1 tbsp Cream Cheese
- 1 ounce shredded Cheese by choice

Method:

1. Preheat and grease the sandwich maker with cooking spray.
2. Cut the muffin in half and spread the cream cheese over its insides.
3. Place one half on top of the bottom ring, with the cream cheese side up.
4. Arrange the apple slices on top.
5. Add the pork and top with the cheese.
6. Lower the top ring and cooking plate and place the second half with the cut-side down, there.
7. Close and cook for 4 minutes.
8. Slide out the plate and rotate clockwise.
9. Transfer to a plate and enjoy!

Nutritional Information per Serving:

- Calories 471
- Total Fats 27g
- Carbs 29g
- Protein 28g
- Fiber: 2.5g

Spicy Pork and Pimento Sandwich

Preparation Time: 5 minutes
Cooking Time: 4 minutes
Servings: 1

Ingredients:

- 3 ounces cooked ground Pork
- 1 ounce shredded Pimento Cheese
- 1 tbsp chopped Red Onion
- 1 smaller Hamburger Bun
- 1 ½ tsp Tomato Puree
- ½ tsp Chili Powder

Method:

1. Preheat the sandwich maker and grease it with some cooking spray.
2. Cut the bun in half.
3. When the green light appears, add half of the bun to the bottom ring.
4. Place the pork, red onion, and cheese on top.
5. Sprinkle the chili powder over.
6. Lower the top ring and cooking plate.
7. Top the sandwich with the second half with the cut-side down.
8. Close and cook for 4 minutes.
9. Slide out clockwise, lift it open, and transfer to a plate with a spatula that's not metal.
10. Serve and enjoy!

Nutritional Information per Serving:

- Calories 532
- Total Fats 28.5g
- Carbs 34.4g

- Protein 33g
- Fiber: 1.2g

Hot Pork Sausage and Srambled Egg Sandwich

Preparation Time: 5 minutes

Cooking Time: 4 minutes

Servings: 1

Ingredients:

- 2 ounces ground Pork Sausage, cooked
- 1 ounce shredded Cheddar Cheese
- 1 Egg
- ¼ tsp dried Thyme
- 1 Biscuit
- ½ tsp Hot Pepper Sauce
- Salt and Pepper, to taste

Method:

1. Preheat and grease the sandwich maker with cooking spray.
2. Cut the biscuit in half and place one half inside the bottom ring.
3. Top with the sausage and cheddar, and sprinkle the hot sauce over.
4. Lower the top ring and cooking plate, and crack the egg into it.
5. Season with salt and pepper and sprinkle the thyme over.
6. Close the unit and wait 4 minutes before rotating clockwise to open.
7. Serve and enjoy!

Nutritional Information per Serving:

- Calories 455
- Total Fats 33g
- Carbs 13g
- Protein 26g
- Fiber: 0.4g

Pork and Egg Tortilla Open Sandwich

Preparation Time: 5 minutes
Cooking Time: 4 minutes
Servings: 1

Ingredients:

- 1 Wheat Tortilla
- 1 Egg
- 2 ounces cooked ground Pork
- 1 ounce shredded Cheddar Cheese
- 1 tbsp chopped Red Onion
- 1 tbsp Salsa

Method:

1. Preheat and grease the sandwich maker.
2. Cut the tortilla, if needed, to fit inside the sandwich maker, and then add it to the bottom ring.
3. Place the pork on top of it, sprinkle the cheddar over, and top with the onion.
4. Lower the top ring and crack the egg into it.
5. Close the unit and wait for about 4 minutes before rotating the handle clockwise.
6. Open and transfer to a plate carefully.
7. Top with the salsa.
8. Enjoy!

Nutritional Information per Serving:

- Calories 466
- Total Fats 28.3g
- Carbs 20.5g
- Protein 31g
- Fiber: 1.5g

Veggie and Pork Mayo Sandwich

Preparation Time: 5 minutes
Cooking Time: 3 1/2 minutes
Servings: 1

Ingredients:

- 1 smaller Hamburger Bun
- 1 tbsp shredded Carrots
- 1 tbsp shredded Cabbage
- 1 tbsp chopped Onion
- 1 tsp Pickle Relish
- 1 tbsp Mayonnaise
- 2 ounces chopped cooked Pork
- Salt and Pepper, to taste

Method:

1. Grease the Breakfast Sandwich Maker with cooking spray and preheat it.
2. Cut the hamburger bun in half and brush the mayonnaise over the insides of the bun.
3. Place one of the halves inside the bottom ring, with the cut-side up.
4. Top with the pork and veggies.
5. Season with salt and pepper, and top with the pickle relish.
6. Lower the top ring and add the second half of the bun with the cut-side down.
7. Close the unit and cook for 3 ½ minutes.
8. Rotate the handle clockwise to open.
9. Transfer to a plate and enjoy!

Nutritional Information per Serving:

- Calories 395
- Total Fats 25g

- Carbs 28g
- Protein 20g
- Fiber: 1.5g

Pulled Pork Sandwich

Preparation Time: 5 minutes
Cooking Time: 4 minutes
Servings: 1

Ingredients:

- 1 smaller Hamburger Bun
- 3 ounces Pulled Pork
- 4 Red Onion Rings
- ½ Pickle, sliced
- 2 tsp Mustard

Method:

1. Preheat the sandwich maker and grease it with some cooking spray.
2. Cut the bun in half and spread the insides with the mustard.
3. When the green light appears, place on bu half into the bottom ring with the cut-side up.
4. Top with pork, onion rings, and pickle.
5. Lower the top ring and plate and place the second bun half inside.
6. Close and cook for 4 minutes.
7. Rotate clockwise and open carefully.
8. Serve and enjoy!

Nutritional Information per Serving:

- Calories 372
- Total Fats 18g
- Carbs 27g
- Protein 27g
- Fiber: 2.2g

Chapter 7: Chicken and Turkey Sandwiches

The Ultimate Chicken, Spinach and Mozzarella Sandwich

Preparation Time: 5 minutes
Cooking Time: 4 minutes
Servings: 1

Ingredients:

- 1 small Hamburger Bun
- 3 ounces cooked and chopped Chicken
- 1 tbsp Cream Cheese
- 1 ounce shredded Mozzarella
- 1 tbsp canned Corn
- 2 tbsp chopped Spinach

Method:

1. Preheat and grease the sandwich maker.
2. Cut the bun in half and brush the cream cheese on the insides.
3. Add one half to the bottom ring, with the cut-side up.
4. Place the chicken on top and top with the spinach, corn, and mozzarella.
5. Lower the top ring and add the second half of the bun, the cut-side down.
6. Cook for 4 minutes.
7. Rotate clockwise and lift to open.
8. Serve and enjoy!

Nutritional Information per Serving:

- Calories 402
- Total Fats 15.5g
- Carbs 32g
- Protein 32.5g

- Fiber: 1.4g

Spicy Turkey and Sausage Sandwich

Preparation Time: 5 minutes
Cooking Time: 4 minutes
Servings: 1

Ingredients:

- 1 ounce cooked ground Turkey
- 4 slices of Spicy Sausage
- 2 tsp Salsa
- ¼ tsp Cumin
- 1 tbsp refined Beans
- 1 tsp Sour Cream
- 1 tbsp shredded Cheddar Cheese
- 2 small Tortillas

Method:

1. Preheat the sandwich maker and grease it with some cooking spray.
2. Cut the tortillas into circles so they can fit inside the unit.
3. Add one tortilla on top of the bottom ring and spread half of the salsa over.
4. Top with the turkey and sausage, and sprinkle the cumin over.
5. Add the beans and cheese, and drizzle the sour cream over.
6. Brush the remaining salsa on the second tortilla and place it on top of the cheese with the salsa-side down.
7. Close the unit and cook for 4 minutes.
8. Lift it open and transfer to a plate carefully.
9. Serve and enjoy!

Nutritional Information per Serving:

- Calories 470
- Total Fats 26g

- Carbs 32g
- Protein 26g
- Fiber: 3g

Chicken and Bacon Paprika Sandwich

Preparation Time: 5 minutes
Cooking Time: 4 minutes
Servings: 1

Ingredients:

- 1 ounce ground Chicken
- 1 ounce cooked and crumbled Bacon
- ¼ tsp smoked Paprika
- 2 Red Pepper Rings
- 1 slice of Cheese
- 1 tsp chopped Onion
- 2 tsp Dijon Mustard
- 1 small Hamburger Bun

Method:

1. Preheat the sandwich maker until the green light appears and grease it with some cooking spray.
2. Cut the hamburger bun in half and brush the insides with the mustard.
3. Place one half with the mustard-side up, on top of the bottom ring.
4. Add the chicken and bacon and sprinkle the paprika over.
5. Top with the pepper, onion, and add the cheese on top.
6. Lower the top ring and finish it off by adding the second bun, placed with the mustard-side down.
7. Close the lid and cook for 4 minutes.
8. Open the lid with mittens, and carefully transfer to a plate.
9. Serve and enjoy!

Nutritional Information per Serving:

- Calories 298

- Total Fats 13g
- Carbs 21g
- Protein 23.5g
- Fiber: 5.5g

Pita Bread Chicken Sandwich

Preparation Time: 5 minutes

Cooking Time: 3 minutes

Servings: 1

Ingredients:

- 3 ounces shredded Rotisserie Chicken
- ¼ tsp Curry Powder
- 2 tsp Mayonnaise
- 1 tbsp chopped Red Pepper
- 1 tbsp chopped Celery
- 1 tbsp chopped Tomatoes
- 1 tsp chopped Parsley
- 2 small Pita Breads or one large cut into two circles that fit inside the sandwixh maker

Method:

1. Grease the unit with cooking spray and preheat it until the green light appears.
2. Place one pita bread on top of the bottom ring.
3. Add some mayo to it and sprinkle the curry powder over.
4. Top with the chicken, veggies, ad parsley.
5. Drizzle the rest of the mayonnaise.
6. Lower the cooking plate and top ring, and then top the sandwich with the second pita bread.
7. Close and cook the sandwich for 3 minutes.
8. Rotate clockwise and lift to open.
9. Serve and enjoy!

Nutritional Information per Serving:

- Calories 420

- Total Fats 26g
- Carbs 26.5g
- Protein 24g
- Fiber: 3g

Turkey Salsa Melt

Preparation Time: 5 minutes

Cooking Time: 4 minutes

Servings: 1

Ingredients:

- 2 ounces leftover Turkey, chopped up nicely
- 1 English Muffin
- 1 tbsp Salsa
- 1 ounce shredded Cheese by choice
- 1 tsp chopped Celery

Method:

1. Preheat and grease the sandwich maker.
2. Cut the muffin in half and place one half on top of the bottom ring, with the cut-size up.
3. Combine the turkey and salsa and place on top of the muffin.
4. Add the celery on top and sprinkle the cheese over.
5. Lower the top ring and add the second half with he cut-size down.
6. Close and cook for 4 minutes.
7. Carefully open the lid and transfer to a plate.
8. Serve and enjoy!

Nutritional Information per Serving:

- Calories 410
- Total Fats 22g
- Carbs 21g
- Protein 20g
- Fiber: 0.9g

Ground Turkey Taco Cups

Preparation Time: 5 minutes
Cooking Time: 5 minutes
Servings: 1

Ingredients:

- 1 Flour Tortilla
- 1 ounce shredded Cheddar
- 1 tsp Sour Cream
- 1 tsp Salsa
- 2 ounces cooked Ground Chicken
- 2 tsp chopped Onion
- 1 tsp chopped Parsley

Method:

1. Preheat and grease the sandwich maker.
2. Slide out the cooking plate – you will not need it for this recipe.
3. Place the tortilla into the ring, tucking it, so that it looks like a cup.
4. In a small bowl, combine the rest of the ingredients.
5. Fill the taco cup with the chicken filling.
6. Close the lid and cook for 5 minutes.
7. Rotate clockwise and lift to open, then transfer to a plate.
8. Serve and enjoy!

Nutritional Information per Serving:

- Calories 305
- Total Fats 14.5g
- Carbs 19.6g
- Protein 23.2g
- Fiber: 1.3g

Cheesy Chicken Waffle Sandwich

Preparation Time: 5 minutes

Cooking Time: 4 ½ minutes

Servings: 1

Ingredients:

- A couple of thin cooked Chicken Slices, about 2-3 ounces in total
- 1 slice American or Cheddar Cheese
- 1 Prosciutto Slice
- 2 tomato Slices
- 2 tsp Mayonnaise
- 2 Frozen Waffles

Method:

1. Preheat and grease the sandwich maker.
2. Cut the waffles into 4-inch circles so that they can fit inside the unit.
3. Place on waffle on top of the bottom ring.
4. Add the chicken, place the tomato sliced on top, and spread the mayo over.
5. Top with the prosciutto and finish it off by adding the slice of cheese.
6. Lower the top ring and add the second waffle.
7. Close the unit and cook for 4 ½ minutes.
8. Serve and enjoy!

Nutritional Information per Serving:

- Calories 350
- Total Fats 28g
- Carbs 22g
- Protein 24g
- Fiber: 2g

Moist Leftover Chicken Biscuit

Preparation Time: 5 minutes
Cooking Time: 4 minutes
Servings: 1

Ingredients:

- 1 Biscuit
- 2 ounces Leftover Chicken
- 2 tsp Heavy Cream
- 1 ounce shredded Cheddar Cheese

Method:

1. Preheat the unit and grease it with cooking spray.
2. Cut the biscuit in half and add one half to the bottom ring, cut-side up.
3. Add the chicken and sprinkle the heavy cream over.
4. Top with the cheddar cheese and lower the top ring.
5. Add the second half of the biscuit, this time with the cut-side down, and close the unit.
6. Cook for 4 minutes.
7. Lift the lid and transfer the sandwich to a plate.
8. Serve and enjoy!

Nutritional Information per Serving:

- Calories 280
- Total Fats 16g
- Carbs 12g
- Protein 22g
- Fiber: 0.4g

Chapter 8: Fish and Seafood Sandwiches

Tilapia and Pimento Dijon Sandwich

Preparation Time: 5 minutes
Cooking Time: 3-4 minutes
Servings: 1

Ingredients:

- 2 Bread Slices
- 2 ounces chopped cooked Tilapia Fillet
- 1 slice Pimento Cheese
- 2 tsp Dijon Mustard
- ¼ tsp chopped Parsley

Method:

1. Preheat the sandwich maker and grease it with some cooking spray.
2. Cut the bread slices so they can fit inside the unit, and brush the Dijon over them.
3. Place one bread slice into the bottom ring, with the mustard-side up.
4. Add the tilapia, sprinkle with parsley, and top with cheese.
5. Lower the ring and add the second bread slice, with the mustard-side down.
6. Close the appliance and cook for 3 to 4 minutes.
7. Open carefully and transfer to a plate.
8. Serve and enjoy!

Nutritional Information per Serving:

- Calories 388
- Total Fats 13g
- Carbs 35g
- Protein 29g
- Fiber: 6g

Yogurt and Dill Open Cod Sandwich

Preparation Time: 5 minutes
Cooking Time: 3 minutes
Servings: 1

Ingredients:

- 1 small Pita Bread, about 4 inches
- 3 ounces cooked Cod, chopped
- 1 tbsp Greek Yogurt
- 1 tsp chopped Dill
- ¼ tsp Garlic Powder
- 1 ounce shredded Cheddar Cheese

Method:

1. Preheat the unit until the green light appears. Grease with cooking spray.
2. Add the pita bread to the bottom ring and place the cod on top.
3. Sprinkle with the garlic powder and top with the cheddar.
4. Close the lid and cook for 3 minutes or so.
5. Combine the yogurt and dill.
6. Open the lid carefully and transfer to a plate.
7. Drizzle the yogurt and dill mixture over.
8. Enjoy!

Nutritional Information per Serving:

- Calories 282
- Total Fats 12g
- Carbs 17g
- Protein 26.5g
- Fiber: 0.6g

Tuna and Corn Muffin Sandwich

Preparation Time: 5 minutes
Cooking Time: 3 minutes
Servings: 1

Ingredients:

- 1 Whole Wheat English Muffin
- 2 ounces canned Tuna, drained
- 2 tsp Mayonnaise
- 2 tsp canned Corn
- 2 tsp chopped Tomatoes

Method:

1. Preheat and grease the unit.
2. Cut the English muffin half.
3. When the green light appears, add half of the muffin to the bottom ring.
4. Combine together the tuna, mayonnaise, tomatoes, and corn.
5. Place the tuna mixture on top of the muffin half.
6. Lower the top ring and add the second half of the muffin.
7. Close the unit and cook for 3 minutes.
8. Rotate clockwise and open. Transfer to a plate.
9. Serve and enjoy!

Nutritional Information per Serving:

- Calories 255
- Total Fats 9g
- Carbs 29.5g
- Protein 17g
- Fiber: 5g

Canned Salmon and Bacon Pickle Sandwich

Preparation Time: 5 minutes
Cooking Time: 3-4 minutes
Servings: 1

Ingredients:

- 2 ounces canned Salmon
- 1 Bacon Slice, cooked
- 2 Bread Slices
- 1 ounce shredded Mozzarella Cheese
- 1 tsp Pickle Relish
- ½ Pickle, sliced
- 1 tsp Dijon Mustard
- 1 tsp Tomato Puree

Method:

1. Preheat the sandwich maker and grease it with some cooking spray.
2. Cut the bread slices so they can fit the unit.
3. Brush one of the bread slices with Dijon mustard and place it on top oh the bottom ring, with the mustard-side up.
4. Add the salmon and bacon on top and sprinkle with the relish and tomato puree.
5. Arrange the pickle slices over and top with the mozzarella.
6. Lower the top ring and add the second bread slice.
7. Cover the unit and cook for about 3-4 minutes.
8. Rotate clockwise to open an transfer to a plate.
9. Serve and enjoy!

Nutritional Information per Serving:

- Calories 420
- Total Fats 34g

- Carbs 25g
- Protein 28g
- Fiber: 3.5g

Salmon and Pistachio Melt

Preparation Time: 5 minutes
Cooking Time: 3-4 minutes
Servings: 1

Ingredients:

- 2 Bread Slices
- 2 ounces chopped cooked Salmon
- 2 tsp chopped Pistachios
- 1 ounce shredded Mozzarella

Method:

1. Preheat and grease the sandwich maker with cooking spray.
2. Cut the bread slices into circles so they can fit perfectly inside the unit.
3. Add the first slice to the bottom ring and place the salmon on top.
4. Add the pistachios over and top with the mozzarella.
5. Lower the top ring and add the remaining bread slice.
6. Close and cook for 3-4 minutes.
7. Rotate clockwise and lift open.
8. Transfer to a plate and enjoy!

Nutritional Information per Serving:

- Calories 423
- Total Fats 16g
- Carbs 41g
- Protein 30.8g
- Fiber: 7g

Sour Cream and Crab Cake Sandwich

Preparation Time: 5 minutes
Cooking Time: 3 ½ minutes
Servings: 1

Ingredients:

- 1 frozen Crab Cake Pattie
- 2 tsp Sour Cream
- 1 slice American Cheese
- ½ Pickle, sliced
- 1 Biscuit

Method:

1. Preheat the sandwich maker and grease it with some cooking spray.
2. Cut the biscuit in half and place one half to the bottom ring of the unit.
3. Spread half of the sour cream over and add the crab cake on top.
4. Spread the remaining sour cream over the crab cake, arrange the pickle slices over, and top with the cheese.
5. Lower the top ring and add the second biscuit half.
6. Close the unit and cook for 3 ½ minutes.
7. Open carefully and transfer to a plate.
8. Serve and enjoy!

Nutritional Information per Serving:

- Calories 340
- Total Fats 26g
- Carbs 21g
- Protein 23g
- Fiber: 3g

Fish Finger Sandwich

Preparation Time: 5 minutes
Cooking Time: 4 minutes
Servings: 1

Ingredients:

- 2 Fish Fingers, cooked and chopped
- 1 small Hamburger Bun
- 1 tbsp Cream Cheese
- 1 ounce Cheddar Cheese
- 1 tbsp chopped Red Onion

Method:

1. Preheat the sandwich maker and grease it with some cooking spray.
2. Cut the bun in half and brush it with the cream cheese.
3. Place one half on top of the the bottom ring, with the cream cheese side up.
4. Add the fish finger pieces on top, sprinkle with the red onion and top with the cheddar.
5. Lower the cooking plate and top ring and add the second half of the bun, with the cream cheese down.
6. Close the unit and cook for about 4 minutes.
7. Open carefully and transfer to a plate.
8. Serve and enjoy!

Nutritional Information per Serving:

- Calories 350
- Total Fats 20g
- Carbs 26g
- Protein 22g
- Fiber: 4g

Salsa and Shrimp Biscuit Sandwich

Preparation Time: 5 minutes

Cooking Time: 3 minutes

Servings: 1

Ingredients:

- 4 small Shrimp, cooked
- ½ tbsp Salsa
- 2 tsp Cream Cheese
- 1 ounce shredded Mozzarella Cheese
- 1 Biscuit

Method:

1. Preheat the sandwich maker and grease it with some cooking spray.
2. Cut the biscuit in half and spread the cream cheese over the insides.
3. Add one half of the biscuit to the bottom ring, with the cream cheese up.
4. Top with the shrimp and salsa, and sprinkle the mozzarella cheese over.
5. Lower the top ring and add the second biscuit half, with the cream cheese down.
6. Close the unit and cook for 3 minutes.
7. Rotate clockwise and open carefully.
8. Serve and enjoy!

Nutritional Information per Serving:

- Calories 222
- Total Fats 11g
- Carbs 13g
- Protein 19g
- Fiber: 0.5g

Chapter 9: Gluten-Free Sandwiches

Gluten-Free Crispy Grilled Cheese and Bacon Sandwich

Preparation Time: 5 minutes
Cooking Time: 3 ½ minutes
Servings: 1

Ingredients:

- 1 ounce Bacon, chopped
- 1 ounce shredded Cheddar
- 1 ounce shredded Gouda
- 2 tsp Butter
- 2 Gluten-Free Bread

Method:

1. Preheat the unit until the green light appears. Grease with some cooking spray.
2. Spread the butter over the bread slices, and cut them to make them fit inside the unit.
3. Place one bread slice on top of the bottom ring, with the butter-side down.
4. Top with the cheese and bacon.
5. Lower the top rin and add the second slice of bread, with the butter-side up.
6. Close the lid and cook for 3 ½ minutes.
7. Rotate clockwise, open, and transfer to a plate.
8. Serve and enjoy!

Nutritional Information per Serving:

- Calories 430
- Total Fats 22g
- Carbs 39g
- Protein 20g

- Fiber: 5g

Avocado Sandwich with Egg, Ham and Cheese

Preparation Time: 5 minutes
Cooking Time: 4 minutes
Servings: 1

Ingredients:

- 4 Large Avocado Slices
- 1 Egg
- 1 Ham Slice
- 1 slice American Cheese
- Salt and Pepper, to taste

Method:

1. Preheat the sandwich maker until the green light appears and grease it with cooking spray.
2. Arrange two of the avocado slices on the bottom ring.
3. Place the ham and cheese on top.
4. Lower the cooking plate and crack the egg into it. Season with salt and pepper.
5. Top with the remaining avocado slices.
6. Close the sandwich maker and cook for 4 minutes.
7. Side out and rotate clockwise. Open and transfer the sandwich with a spatula, very carefully, as you are using avocado slices, not bread.
8. Serve and enjoy!

Nutritional Information per Serving:

- Calories 580
- Total Fats 44g
- Carbs 21g
- Protein 28g
- Fiber: 12g

Mexican Gluten-Free Pork Sandwich

Preparation Time: 5 minutes
Cooking Time: 4 minutes
Servings: 1

Ingredients:

- 2 Corn Tortillas
- 2 ounces pulled Pork
- 2 tsp Salsa
- ½ tbsp Beans
- 1 tsp Corn
- 1 Tomato Slice, chopped
- 2 tsp Red Onion
- 2 tbsp shredded Cheddar Cheese

Method:

1. Preheat the sandwich maker and grease it with some cooking spray.
2. Cut the corn tortillas into 4-inch circles to fit inside the unit.
3. Place one tortilla to the bottom ring and place the pork on top.
4. Add the salsa, corn, beans, onion, and tomato, and top with the shredded cheese.
5. Lower the top ring and add the second corn tortilla.
6. Close and cook for 3-4 minutes.
7. Rotate clockwise and open carefully.
8. Transfer to a plate.
9. Serve and enjoy!

Nutritional Information per Serving:

- Calories 360
- Total Fats 25g
- Carbs 21g

- Protein 24g
- Fiber: 5g

Almond Pancake with Egg and Prosciutto

Preparation Time: 5 minutes
Cooking Time: 4 minutes
Servings: 1

Ingredients:

- 2 4-inch Almond Flour Pancakes, fresh or frozen
- 1 Egg
- 1 ounce chopped Prosciutto
- 1 ounce shredded Cheddar
- Salt and Pepper, to taste

Method:

1. Preheat the sandwich maker and grease it with some cooking spray.
2. Add one pancake to the bottom ring and top it with prosciutto and cheddar.
3. Lower the top ring and cooking plate, and crack the egg into it. Season with salt and pepper.
4. Add the second pancake on top and close the unit.
5. Cook for 3 minutes or 4 if using frozen pancakes.
6. Open carefully and transfer to a plate.
7. Serve and enjoy!

Nutritional Information per Serving:

- Calories 430
- Total Fats 34.5g
- Carbs 5.8g
- Protein 25g
- Fiber: 1.3g

Almond Flour Waffle and Sausage Sandwich

Preparation Time: 5 minutes
Cooking Time: 4 minutes
Servings: 1

Ingredients:

- 2 Almond Flour Waffles
- 1 Frozen Sausage Pattie
- 1 slice American Cheese
- 2 Red Onion Rings
- 2 Tomato Slices

Method:

1. Preheat the sandwich maker until the green light appears and grease the unit with cooking spray.
2. Add one waffle to the bottom ring and top with the sausage pattie.
3. Add the tomato slices and red onion over, and place the cheese on top.
4. Lower the top ring and add the second waffle.
5. Close the unit and cook for 4 minutes.
6. Rotate clockwise and open.
7. Serve and enjoy!

Nutritional Information per Serving:

- Calories 345
- Total Fats 28g
- Carbs 14g
- Protein 20g
- Fiber: 7g

Cornbread and Egg Sandwich

Preparation Time: 5 minutes

Cooking Time: 4 minutes

Servings: 1

Ingredients:

- 2 corn-only Cornbread Slices
- 1 Egg
- 1 tbsp shredded Cheddar
- 1 tsp cooked and crumbled Bacon

Method:

1. Preheat the unit and grease it with some cooking spray.
2. Cut the cornbread slcies into rounds so they can fit inside the unit, and place one on top of the bottom ring.
3. Add the cheddar and bacon.
4. Whisk the egg a bit, lower the cooking plate, and add it to it.
5. Place the second cornbread slice on top.
6. Close the sandwich maker and cook for 4 minutes.
7. Slide out and open the lid carefully.
8. Transfer to a plate and enjoy!

Nutritional Information per Serving:

- Calories 320
- Total Fats 17g
- Carbs 24g
- Protein 12g
- Fiber: 4g

Corn Bowl with Tomato, Bacon, and Cheese

Preparation Time: 5 minutes

Cooking Time: 3 ½ minutes

Servings: 1

Ingredients:

- 1 Corn Tortilla
- 1 tbsp chopped Tomatoes
- 2 Basil Slices, chopped
- 1 ounce shredded Cheddar Cheese
- 2 Bacon Slices, chopped

Method:

1. Preheat the sandwich maker and grease it with some cooking spray.
2. Add the corn tortilla to the bottom ring, and press it well inside to make it look like a bowl.
3. Add the rest of the ingredients inside.
4. Close the unit and cook for 3 ½ minutes.
5. Lift up to open and carefully transfer to a plate.
6. Serve and enjoy!

Nutritional Information per Serving:

- Calories 262
- Total Fats 16.4g
- Carbs 13g
- Protein 16g
- Fiber: 1.9g

Gluten-Free Smoked Salmon and Cream Cheese Sandwich

Preparation Time: 5 minutes
Cooking Time: 3 minutes
Servings: 1

Ingredients:

- 1 ounce Smoked Salmon
- 1 tbsp Cream Cheese
- 1 ounce shredded Mozzarella
- 2 gluten-free Bread Slices

Method:

1. Preheat the sandwich maker and grease it with some cooking spray.
2. Cut the bread slices into circles that can fit inside the appliance.
3. When the green light appears, add one bread slice to the bottom ring.
4. Add half of the cream cheese and lightly spread it.
5. Add the smoked salmon and mozzarella on top.
6. Lower the top ring.
7. Spread the remaining cream cheese over the second bread slice.
8. Place the bread slice on top, with the cream cheese down.
9. Close the unit and cook for 3 minutes.
10. Rotate clockwise to open.
11. Serve and enjoy!

Nutritional Information per Serving:

- Calories 348
- Total Fats 14.6g
- Carbs 39g
- Protein 15g
- Fiber: 5g

Chapter 10: Beef Sandwiches and Burgers

Classic Hamburger

Preparation Time: 5 minutes
Cooking Time: 4 ½ minutes
Servings: 1

Ingredients:

- 1 smaller Hamburger Bun
- 1 frozen Beef Pattie
- 1 tsp Dijon Mustard
- 1 tsp chopped Onion
- 1 tsp chopped Tomato

Method:

1. Preheat the sandwich maker and grease it with some cooking spray.
2. Cut the hamburger bun in half, and place one half on top of the bottom ring, with the cut-side up.
3. Place the pattie on top and brush the mustard over.
4. Sprinkle with the tomato and onion.
5. Lower the top ring and add the second half of the bun
6. Close the unit and cook for 4 ½ minutes, not less, because you are using frozen pattie.
7. Rotate clockwise and open carefully.
8. Serve and enjoy!

Nutritional Information per Serving:

- Calories 383
- Total Fats 23g
- Carbs 26.6g

- Protein 25g
- Fiber: 0.1g

Beef and Veggies Bagel Sandwich

Preparation Time: 5 minutes
Cooking Time: 3 minutes
Servings: 1

Ingredients:

- 1 tsp canned Peas
- 1 tsp canned Corn
- 1 tsp chopped Celery
- 1 tsp chopped Onion
- 1 Tomato Slice, chopped
- 2 ounces cooked Beef Roast, chopped
- 1 tbsp Sandwich Sauce
- 1 tbsp Cream Cheese
- 1 Bagel

Method:

1. Preheat the sandwich maker and grease it with some cooking spray.
2. Cut the bagel in half and spread the cream cheese over.
3. Place one half of the bagel on top of the bottom ring, with the spread-side up.
4. Top with the beef and veggies, and drizzle the sauce over.
5. Lower the top ring and add the second bagel half inside, with the cream cheese down.
6. Close the lid and cook for 3 minutes.
7. Rotate clockwise and open carefully.
8. Serve and enjoy!

Nutritional Information per Serving:

- Calories 420
- Total Fats 25g

- Carbs 28g
- Protein 23g
- Fiber: 5g

Chili Sandwich

Preparation Time: 5 minutes
Cooking Time: 3 – 3 ½ inutes
Servings: 1

Ingredients:

- 2 ounces cooked ground Beef
- 1 English Muffin
- ¼ tsp Chili Powder
- 1 tbsp chopped Tomatoes
- 2 tsp Beans

Method:

1. Grease your Breakfast Sandwich Maker and preheat it.
2. Cut the muffin in half.
3. When the green light appears, add one muffin half with the cut-side down, to the bottom ring.
4. In a small bowl, combine the tomatoes, beans, chili powder, and beef.
5. Top the muffin half with the beef mixture.
6. Lower the top ring and add the second muffin half.
7. Close the lid and cook for 3 to 3 ½ minutes.
8. Open carefully and transfer to a plate.
9. Serve and enjoy!

Nutritional Information per Serving:

- Calories 320
- Total Fats 16g
- Carbs 28g
- Protein 15g
- Fiber: 3g

Sausage and Biscuit

Preparation Time: 5 minutes
Cooking Time: 4 minutes
Servings: 1

Ingredients:

- 1 Frozen Beef Sausage Patty
- 1 Biscuit
- 1 tbsp Gravy
- 1 slice Cheese
- 1 Egg, lightly beaten
- Salt and Pepper

Method:

1. Preheat the unit until the green light appears. Grease with cooking spray.
2. Cut the biscuit in half and place one on top of the bottom ring.
3. Add the patty and top with the cheese.
4. Lower the cooking plate and add the egg to it. Season with salt and pepper.
5. Close the lid and cook for at least 4 minutes.
6. Rotate clockwise and lift to open.
7. Transfer to a plate and drizzle the gravy over.
8. Serve and enjoy!

Nutritional Information per Serving:

- Calories 410
- Total Fats 35g
- Carbs 21g
- Protein 29g
- Fiber: 3g

Bolognese Cup

Preparation Time: 5 minutes
Cooking Time: 3 ½ minutes
Servings: 1

Ingredients:

- 1 Flour Tortilla
- 2 ounces ground Beef, cooked
- 1 tsp chopped Onion
- 1 tbsp Marinara Sauce
- 1 ounce shredded Mozzarella Cheese

Method:

1. Preheat the sandwich maker and grease it with some cooking spray.
2. Add the tortilla inside, tucking it in, until it looks like a cup.
3. Add the beef, onion, and marinara sauce inside. Stir a bit to combine.
4. Top with the shredded mozzarella cheese.
5. Close the sandwich maker and cook for 3 ½ minutes.
6. Open the lid and transfer to a plate.
7. Serve and enjoy!

Nutritional Information per Serving:

- Calories 375
- Total Fats 24g
- Carbs 20g
- Protein 19g
- Fiber: 1.4g

Beef, Waffle, and Egg Sandwich

Preparation Time: 5 minutes
Cooking Time: 4 minutes
Servings: 1

Ingredients:

- 1 frozen Beef Pattie
- 2 4-inch Waffles
- 1 Egg, whisked
- ¼ tsp Garlic Powder
- Salt and Pepper, to taste
- 1 slice Cheddar Cheese

Method:

1. Preheat the unit until the green light appears. Grease with cooking spray.
2. Add one waffle to the bottom ring.
3. Add the beef pattie on top and top with the cheddar.
4. Lower the cooking plate and add the egg to it. Season with salt, pepper, and garlic powder.
5. Close the unit and cook for 4 minutes, not less.
6. Rotate the handles clockwise, lift to open, and carefully transfer to a plate.
7. Serve and enjoy!

Nutritional Information per Serving:

- Calories 562
- Total Fats 38g
- Carbs 28g
- Protein 38g
- Fiber: 3g

Cheesy Beef and Egg Sandwich

Preparation Time: 5 minutes
Cooking Time: 4 minutes
Servings: 1

Ingredients:

- 2 ounces cooked ground Beef
- 2 Bread Slices
- 1 Egg
- 1 ounce shredded Cheddar
- 1 tsp Mayonnaise
- Salt and Pepper, to taste

Method:

1. Preheat the sandwich maker until the green light appears, and grease it with some cooking spray.
2. Cut the bread slices so they can fit inside the sandwich maker, and place one on top of the bottom ring.
3. Add the beef and cheddar and lower the top ring and cooking plate.
4. Crack the egg into the plate and season it with salt and pepper.
5. Brush the second slices with the mayo and place it with the mayo-side down.
6. Close the lid and cook for 4 minutes.
7. Slide out the cooking plate and open the lid carefully.
8. Tranfer to a plate with a spatula that is not metal.
9. Serve and enjoy!

Nutritional Information per Serving:

- Calories 590
- Total Fats 35g
- Carbs 38g

- Protein 31g
- Fiber: 6g

The Ultimate 4-Minute Cheeseburger

Preparation Time: 5 minutes

Cooking Time: 4 minutes

Servings: 1

Ingredients:

- 1 frozen Beef Patty
- 1 small Hamburger Bun
- 1 slice American Cheese
- 1 ounce cooked and crumbled Bacon
- 1 tsp Pickle Relish
- 2 Tomato Slices
- 1 tsp Dijon Mustard

Method:

1. Preheat the sandwich maker and grease it with some cooking spray.
2. Cut the bun in half and place one on top of the bottom ring.
3. Add the patty on top and brush with the mustard.
4. Top with bacon, pickle relish, and tomato slices.
5. Place the cheese on top.
6. Lower the top ring and add the second bun half.
7. Close the unit and cook for 4 minutes.
8. Open carefully and transfer to a plate.
9. Serve and enjoy!

Nutritional Information per Serving:

- Calories 480
- Total Fats 31g
- Carbs 24g
- Protein 28g

- Fiber: 2g

Chapter 11: Desserts and Snacks

Chocolate Croissant

Preparation Time: 5 minutes
Cooking Time: 3 minutes
Servings: 1

Ingredients:

- 2 ounces Chocolate, chopped
- 1 Croissant
- 1 tsp Heavy Cream

Method:

1. Preheat the sandwich maker and grease it with some cooking spray.
2. Cut the croissant in half and place one half on top of the bottom ring, with the cut-side up.
3. Arrange the chocolate pieces on top and sprinkle with the heavy cream.
4. Lower the top ring and add the second croissant part, with the cut-side down.
5. Cook for 3 minutes.
6. Open carefully and transfer to a plate.
7. Serve and enjoy!

Nutritional Information per Serving:

- Calories 283
- Total Fats 14g
- Carbs 32g
- Protein 6g
- Fiber: 1.8g

Crunchy Nutella and Strawberry Bagel

Preparation Time: 5 minutes
Cooking Time: 3 minutes
Servings: 1

Ingredients:

- ½ Bagel
- 1 tbsp Nutella
- 4 Strawberries, sliced
- 1 tsp chopped Hazelnuts

Method:

1. Preheat the Breakfast Sandwich Maker until the green light appears. Spray with some cooking spray.
2. Spread the Nutella over the bagel.
3. Place the bagel on top of the bottom ring, with the cut-side up.
4. Arrange the strawberry slices over, and sprinkle with the hazelnuts.
5. Close the lid and cook for 3 minutes.
6. Rotate the handle clockwise to open.
7. Serve and enjoy!

Nutritional Information per Serving:

- Calories 220
- Total Fats 8g
- Carbs 32g
- Protein 5.8g
- Fiber: 2.2g

Berry Pancake

Preparation Time: 5 minutes
Cooking Time: 3 – 4 minutes
Servings: 1

Ingredients:

- 1 Frozen Pancake
- ¼ cup chopped frozen Berries
- 1 tsp Sugar
- 1 tbsp Whipped Cream

Method:

1. Preheat the sandwich maker and grease it with some cooking spray.
2. Place the pancake on top of the bottom ring.
3. Arrange the berries over and sprinkle with the sugar.
4. Close the lid and cook for 3 – 4 minutes.
5. Open carefully and transfer to a plate.
6. Top with the whipped cream and enjoy!

Nutritional Information per Serving:

- Calories 117
- Total Fats 2g
- Carbs 23g
- Protein 2.3g
- Fiber: 2g

Peanut Butter Waffle with Banana

Preparation Time: 5 minutes
Cooking Time: 4 minutes
Servings: 1

Ingredients:

- 1 Frozen Waffle
- 1 tbsp Peanut Butter
- ¼ Banana, sliced

Method:

1. Preheat the sandwich maker and grease it with some cooking spray.
2. Place the waffle on top of the bottom ring.
3. Spread the peanut butter over and close the lid.
4. Cook for about 3 minutes.
5. Open carefully and transfer to a plate.
6. Top with the banana slices and enjoy!

Nutritional Information per Serving:

- Calories 214
- Total Fats 11g
- Carbs 25g
- Protein 6.3g
- Fiber: 2.9g

Olive and Cheese Snack

Preparation Time: 5 minutes
Cooking Time: 3 minutes
Servings: 1

Ingredients:

- 1 Bread Slice
- 1 ounce Shredded Cheese
- 1 Basil Leaf, chopped
- 2 Kalamata Olives, diced

Method:

1. Grease the unit and preheat it until the green light appears.
2. Cut the bread slice so that it can fit inside the unit, and place it on top of the bottom ring.
3. Top with the olives, basil, and cheese.
4. Close the lid and cook for 3 minutes.
5. Rotate clockwise and open carefully.
6. Transfer with a non-metal spatula and enjoy!

Nutritional Information per Serving:

- Calories 205
- Total Fats 12.7g
- Carbs 15g
- Protein 10g
- Fiber: 2.1g

Cinnamon Apple Biscuit

Preparation Time: 5 minutes
Cooking Time: 4 minutes
Servings: 1

Ingredients:

- 2 tbsp grated Apple
- ¼ tsp Cinnamon
- ½ Biscuit
- ½ tsp Sugar

Method:

1. Preheat the sandwich maker and grease the insides with cooking spray.
2. Add the biscuit with the cut-side up, to the bottom ring of the unit.
3. Top with the grated apple and sprinkle the sugar and cinnamon over.
4. Close the unit and cook for 3 minutes.
5. Open carefully and transfer to a plate.
6. Serve and enjoy!

Nutritional Information per Serving:

- Calories 55
- Total Fats 0.6g
- Carbs 12.2g
- Protein 1g
- Fiber: 1.2g

Pizza Snack

Preparation Time: 5 minutes
Cooking Time: 4 minutes
Servings: 1

Ingredients:

- ½ English Muffin
- 4 mini Pepeproni Slices
- 1 tbsp shredded Cheddar Cheese
- 1 tsp Ketchup

Method:

1. Preheat the unit until the green light appears and grease it with cooking spray.
2. Add the muffin to the bottom ring.
3. Spread the ketchup over it and top with the pepperoni and cheese.
4. Close the lid and cook for 3 minutes.
5. Open carefully and transfer to a plate with a non-metal spatula.
6. Serve and enjoy!

Nutritional Information per Serving:

- Calories 197
- Total Fats 11.7g
- Carbs 14g
- Protein 8.5g
- Fiber: 1g

Tropical Croissant with Sugar

Preparation Time: 5 minutes
Cooking Time: 4 minutes
Servings: 1

Ingredients:

- 1 tbsp mashed canned Pineapple
- 1 tbsp Mango chunks
- 1 tsp Butter
- ½ Croissant
- 1 tsp Powdered Sugar

Method:

1. Preheat the unit and grease it with cooking spray.
2. Spread the butter over the croissant, and place on top of the bottom ring, with the butter-side down.
3. Top with the pineapple and mango chunks.
4. Close the lid and cook for 3 minutes.
5. Rotate clockwise, and lift to open carefully.
6. Transfer to a plate and sprinkle with the powdered sugar.
7. Enjoy!

Nutritional Information per Serving:

- Calories 194
- Total Fats 10g
- Carbs 24.6g
- Protein 2.6g
- Fiber: 1.3g

Conclusion

Looking for the best breakfast recipes for your Mediterranean breakfast sandwich maker? Then you have found the best book in the world. The best part about the recipes is that you can make these breakfast in just a few minutes. Besides, the most important point is to choose the right ingredients so that the flavors can combine perfectly with the crispiness of the bread.

If you're looking for delicious Mediterranean breakfast recipes that are not too complicated and are budget-friendly - this cookbook is for you. This cookbook is an invaluable and delicious collection of healthy Mediterranean breakfast recipes that will please everyone at the table and become all-time favorites.

Get this book today and start your Mediterranean breakfast journey!

www.ingramcontent.com/pod-product-compliance
Lightning Source LLC
Chambersburg PA
CBHW081404070526
44583CB00020B/2667